The Little Book of Freelance Writing

Writing ideas, opportunities, inspiration and success stories

By Susie Kearley

About the Author

Susie Kearley is a British freelance writer and journalist, working for magazines, newspapers, and book publishers around the world. Among her best known clients are the BBC, IPC Media, and DC Thomson. She has two other books on writing available: 'Freelance Writing: Aim Higher, Earn More' and 'Freelance Writing On Health, Food and Gardens'.

Dedication

This book is dedicated to all the aspiring freelance writers who tried and failed to get published, picked themselves up, and tried again... and again. If you're still doing that, chin up, keep going, do courses if you need to, and hone your skills. If you're published and on a roll, well done!

CHAPTERS   Page

Chapter 1
Introduction

Let me introduce myself. I am a full-time freelance writer, embarking on my sixth year trading. I make a good income writing for magazines and newspapers across the English speaking world. I also write some articles for corporate clients.

I started working as a freelance writer after taking redundancy from a career in marketing. A short-term job working for a marketing agency opened my eyes to the opportunities in freelance writing, as they used freelancers to write their clients' brochures. The lifestyle appealed, and I'd harboured writing ambitions for many years, so I took the plunge. I was also much more capable and conscientious than some of the freelance writers that this company was using, which gave me confidence. I didn't work for that company, but I did find many other clients. Getting started was hard work, but I've never looked back and I'm really glad I did it.

I started pitching article ideas to the editors of magazines that I wanted to write for - all day long, relentlessly. I got rejection after rejection initially - and those that didn't reject me, offered 'exposure' in return for working for free. Well I was serious about a career, so 'exposure' wasn't enough. I needed to chase the money.

Among those offering 'exposure' was a glossy women's magazine called Marie Claire. I agreed to cooperate with a short interview piece for Marie Claire, just so that I could say I'd been published by that magazine (on their website). But as a general rule, I was very focused on the money. I had to be. I'd quit my job, and this was supposed to be my new career!

My first paid commission came from a military magazine, followed by a couple of assignments from gardening magazines and I was away! I kept pitching relentlessly, and the work kept coming in. The rest is history.

Building your portfolio

Among my first regular assignments was a column in the local newspaper about events happening in my town. That kind of opportunity is a reasonable starting point - it gets you focused on the writing discipline, meeting deadlines, developing a routine, ensuring a high level of accuracy, and complying with in-house style-guides.

I'd also had some work published in a regional magazine some years earlier, which meant that when I started writing full-time, I had a modest portfolio of work to show off. I did those early articles for free because it was promoting something that was in my interests - a part-time business venture. Doing the odd thing for free can help you get a basic portfolio together and give you credibility when you start pitching for paid work.

Handling rejection

It can be very easy to give up in the face of rejection, but if you want to be published badly enough, you'll need to keep plugging away, and improve your craft until you get there.

When I got started, I read lots of books, asked people for advice, and persevered. I pitched feature ideas all day, every day, for weeks before I got a positive reply. Tenacity and determination really help - but you've got to have a good command of English and some decent ideas too.

Look around for ideas, speak to people, visit interesting places, and look for inspiration in your every day life. You'll be surprised how many story ideas there are all around you when you get into the habit of doing this.

Making contacts

A common problem for all new writers is a lack of contacts, and we all have to start somewhere. The Writers' and Artists' Yearbook, a magazine's website, or the editorial column inside a magazine itself, are all good places to start. Staff turnover can be quite high in publishing, so it's worth checking the current position online if in doubt.

Agents

Do you need an agent? No. I don't have an agent. I've now received two book contracts directly with two different publishers. So I don't think you need one. However, securing an agent can be very helpful if you have your heart set on a publishing deal with a large publishing house, and it may also be more important if you're planning to write a novel and want to achieve global success.

Agents represent your interests. They can, hopefully, get your manuscript in front of the people who matter and get you a decent advance. Getting access to the big publishers is very difficult to achieve without an agent, as most of them refuse to deal directly with authors these days. So it's when you're seeking access to the big publishers that having an agent can be very useful indeed.

You can find a list of agents, and their specialisms, in the Writers' and Artists' Yearbook. Be sure to target those who deal in your specific genre or specialism, rather than taking a scattergun approach to contacting them.

The challenges

Since starting my writing career, there have been a number of challenges to overcome. The first is getting enough work to make it a full-time career, but that comes with time, perseverence, and dedication.

Getting paid quickly is another of the biggest challenges, and it helps if you have a partner with a regular income or savings to keep you afloat when money's tight.

Freelance writers often don't get paid until their article is published, which depending on the publication, can take months, or even years. There are also issues with many publications having their budgets cut at the moment, so some are cutting their fees, and others are taking less freelance material. It's a real squeeze.

As a freelancer, it can be useful to have other skills, which enable you to diversify. I intend to do more on the photography side in the future, and I hope to do more writing for business markets, where you typically get paid more quickly.

Top tips for freelance writers
- Persevere.
- Take notice of all feedback because it often

provides valuable insight into how you can improve your writing skills.

- Read books on writing.
- Meet others who write, for inspiration and support.

Chapter 2
Ideas and inspiration

Inspiration can come from many different places. Last year I did an interview for a pet magazine with author Kate Long, about the guinea pigs that occupy her writing room, her vandal hamster, and her water vole conservation work. Kate's pets provide companionship - the guinea pigs live in her writing office when they're not devouring the lawn - and they inspire her work.

"Some of my books have animals in them," Kate explained, "There's a hedgehog theme in *Before She Was Mine*, a trickster hamster in *Mothers and Daughters*, and in my latest book, *Something Only We Know*, a hamster plays a key role in the plot. I also blog about water voles on www.staggsbrook. blogspot.co.uk".

Like Kate, I take inspiration from pets, people, and other everyday things. Among my earliest sales to magazines were articles for Dogs Monthly, Guinea Pig Magazine, and Popular Fish Keeping. Animals can be a rich source of inspiration and ideas, whether you write fiction or non-fiction.

Travel can be another great source of ideas. Getting away to somewhere new can free your imagination. People you meet might inspire fictional characters, and you can immerse yourself in different cultures and locations, which can be sources of inspiration too. You might come away with ideas for articles on travel, culture, food, interviews, or even personal insight stories.

I've written about travel locations from stately

homes to war museums, to exotic locations abroad. I've even written about my home town as a potential travel destination for other people. When you travel, always take a notebook and look for interesting or unusual things that could become the basis of a good story.

Look for inspiration in your work too. You might think that work is really boring, but at the start of my writing career, I wrote a number of articles for education journals. I'd been working in the education sector for many years. There were some obvious things I could write about with a degree of inside knowledge that editors valued. Don't dismiss subjects like your work as sources of stories. They might seem boring to you, but there may be opportunities to write non-fiction articles for your industry, or to set a piece of fiction in the workplace.

Other sources of inspiration can be conversations with friends and colleagues, wildlife conservation initiatives, local church activities, regional news and press releases, opinion pieces on current affairs, or even hard news, if that's your thing.

Life is full of stories, you just need to develop the writers' instinct to spot a good story when you come across one. And that comes with practice.

Writing groups

Writing groups can be a great source of inspiration. My writing group welcomes a wide variety of interesting speakers, from magazine editors, to performance poets, to children's authors. Many of the speakers share their own ideas and experiences, and try to inspire the group by setting tasks or exercises.

When a very successful romantic comedy author

came to speak to our writing group, she said she got ideas from everyday life. Her books were inspired by her experiences, by people she knew, by conversations she'd had, and even from stories she'd read in the tabloid press. Chats with her friends provided sources of inspiration, and she asked if she could use the ideas in a book. She also said she reads widely across different genres, and had tried experimenting with different writing styles.

Being flexible and trying new things is a good way to find inspiration and discover new interests. I submitted my first poem to a publisher after being inspired to write it by a speaker at my local writers' group.

I've interviewed some of the authors from my writing group for magazine articles too. It's useful to have contacts with interesting stories, and people with whom you can exchange ideas, get feedback, and hear about new writing opportunities.

It also helps to keep life interesting. Some of my recent articles were inspired by new experiences. I enrolled on a FutureLearn course and then wrote about it for a magazine. I've visited museums and written about them for a number of magazines and websites. I even sold an article about the wildlife in Regents Park to a general interest magazine after spending an afternoon there with my camera admiring the flowerbeds and reading about in their wildlife conservation initiatives.

Writing about life

Prolific author Mary Mackie, from Norfolk, is best known for her books about life at Felbrigg Hall, a National Trust property in Norfolk, where she lived with her husband, Chris.

Her humorous accounts of life at the stately home were first published over 20 years ago and two of the books are still in print. Mary has now been writing professionally for 45 years, and has over 70 published books to her name.

Mary's work is inspired by what's going on around her. When her husband Chris was appointed as the new property manager of Felbrigg Hall, she was very involved. "I worked as a room guide, in the shop, and on the ticket desk," she says. "I even ran the tea room for a while. With so much happening all around us, I decided to write about it.

"The book, titled 'Cobwebs and Cream Teas' became a best seller. "It resulted in a lot of publicity and Chris and I went on TV. I wrote a sequel called 'Dry Rot and Daffodils', and then a third called 'Frogspawn and Floor Polish'!"

Mary's humorous accounts of life at Felbrigg Hall became her best known works. The couple lived at Felbrigg between 1983 and 1990. "The highlight was the day Prince Charles visited when the house was shut up for the winter," she says. "We gave him a private tour!

"Life at Felbrigg Hall was full of frustrations and worries, but also of unexpected delights and moments of pure magic," says Mary. Her books are filled with insight, humour, and irony, with tales of rotting timbers, bats and basements, all while they were trying to keep the place spick and span.

Sadly, Chris died in 2014, but not before Mary had documented his life story in her newest full-length book, 'Chris', which was published in 2012.

Chris's story of childhood loss and abandonment,

of being evacuated during the war and eventually being united with his extended family, is brought to life with humour, passion, and all the vigour of a young survivor, picking himself up from hard times, to make the best of what life has to offer.

"I'm immensely glad that he lived to see a happy ending to his personal story," says Mary.

Taking inspiration from the classics

Earlier this year, I interviewed the authors of *A Guinea Pig Oliver Twist*, which combines the classic Dickens tale with guinea pigs dressed up as the characters. The project was inspired by one of the sales team at Bloomsbury Publishing, who came into work with a photograph of their family guinea pig dressed in a Father Christmas hat. The staff loved it.

The photograph sowed the seed of an idea for a series of guinea pig picture books, and they produced the first title in time for Christmas, entitled *A Guinea Pig Nativity*.

The book was a huge hit, selling over 50,000 copies and getting fantastic feedback. Spurred on by this initial success, the next titles were A Guinea Pig Pride & Prejudice, released in autumn 2015, and A Guinea Pig Oliver Twist, released in October 2016. They were all inspired by one picture of a guinea pig in a hat! Who'd have thought!

Tips for generating ideas and inspiration:

- Read widely
- Meet new and interesting people
- Try new things
- Join clubs - perhaps a writers' group!

15

- Travel to new places
- Explore different genres
- Keep abreast of current affairs
- Let your imagination run wild
- Think widely and never tell yourself any idea is stupid. It might just need work.
- Keep an ideas log. It might inspire you later.
- Read writing books.
- Do courses and meet with other writers.
- These things can help to keep your interest alive and your imagination fresh.

Chapter 3
Writing a good pitch

Why should you pitch a feature idea to the editor of a magazine, newspaper, or website, rather than just write it up and send it in?

Editors are busy people and most of them simply don't have the time to read whole articles sent 'on spec'. It's a good idea to send them your idea first, because otherwise you can waste a lot of time writing articles that no-one wants to buy.

Sometimes I have the most amazing ideas, but no-one wants to buy them. It's hard trying to second-guess what editors will like. Often they've published something similar recently, don't feel it's right for them, or have something similar on file to use in the future. So don't write your article 'on spec' unless you know that the publication you're targeting welcomes completed articles sent for consideration.

Writing short fiction is a little different to feature writing. With fiction, you usually *do* have to write the whole story on spec. Do study the magazine's style and submission guidelines before you start writing, so you get the length right and have a greater chance of acceptance. If you're interested in writing full-length books, then you usually have to write the first (or the first three) chapter(s) and a synopsis.

But let's get back to writing articles and composing that perfect pitch. How do you write a winning pitch that results in a sale? Keep the pitch short, straight to the point, and explain why you are the best person for the job. If you haven't grabbed the editor's attention in the first two sentences, you've

17

probably lost them for good.

Briefly outline your idea and explain why your experience, your contacts and interviewees make you the best person to write the article. It should be topical, timely, of interest to their readership, and have a new or unusual slant, so it's less likely to be considered 'old hat' or something they've 'covered before'. It can be helpful to answer the following questions:

- What's the story and why is it important to their readership?
- Home in on individual story, perhaps one person's experience (how this therapy saved my life), rather than the broader topic (an article about this therapy).
- Why should the story be told now/soon? Perhaps it's related to something in the news, something that's trending on social media, or it's related to a newly published study. Perhaps it's seasonal or related to a big anniversary.
- Why are you the best person to write the story? Outline your experience, expertise, contacts.
- Can you supply photos?

If you don't hear back, there could be any number of reasons, so don't take it personally. Editors are very busy and your query may have just been overlooked. Follow up in a couple of weeks if you like. Following up on your ideas can result in unexpected sales.

To give you a feel for a good pitch, some of my successful pitches are shown below. They all resulted in sales. Some are even a bit long. If you can get your idea across in a few lines, do!

How to harness the full potential of social media
Commissioned by ASCL Leader magazine

I wonder if you'd be interested in how schools and colleges are using social media to engage with students? I'd look at best practice, what schools could learn from other public sector bodies about using social media, and how to respond to negativity. I have a background in education marketing and am CIM qualified.

St. Peter's Hospital in Helena says there's nothing like competitions to grow your following on Facebook. A beautiful baby competition saw their following explode from 80 to over 1000.

Bucks New University uses their Facebook group as a discussion forum for students to share their successes, find new house mates, and report good news. They share photos, comments, laughs and problems. There's a real community feel.

I'd detail how to handle negative comments in a positive way, how to use humour to increase your following, and how to identify content that students value. I'd explain how social media is an extension of good customer service, and explain why you need to give up control and listen to feedback.

Herbs of Eden
Commissioned by Kindred Spirit magazine

The Eden Project in Cornwall grows plants from every continent, but what you don't expect to see when you visit this thriving tourist attraction, is a plot of illegal drugs! So imagine our amusement at seeing a hillside of cannabis plants next to the Tropical Biome (low drug content and licenced apparently), and then to stumble across the opiates used to produce heroin near the environmental exhibition!

For those interested in where our modern day remedies come from, both herbal and pharmaceutical, there are some enlightening plants growing in this former quarry. I'd like to take you on a tour of some of them.

Opium Poppy is an ancient source of morphine, codeine and heroin. It is farmed under licence to produce diamorphine (heroin) for medicine, where it is used in hospitals as a pain killer. Codeine in over the counter pain killers is also an opioid drug, producing only morphine, the precursor to heroin.

There are some interesting herbal and medical plants to draw on, including Elecampane, Fewerfew, Evening Primrose, Fox Glove and Black Cohosh. I have photographs.

I would detail a lot more about the health benefits of each plant, and which part of the plant is used as a remedy. I am a qualified nutritionist and have a background in health, enabling me to write with authority on this subject.

Caravan evangelism
Commissioned by Inspire magazine

Chilterns Christian Fellowship has seen good growth after taking innovative approaches to local evangelism. When Reverend Geoff Blease joined the church around 10 years ago, disenchanted youth were hanging around the pretty market town in dark corners, drinking and causing trouble.

So Geoff and his parishioners took to the streets in

a caravan called *The Ark*, inviting young people in for a cup of tea and a chat. *The Ark* made a big difference to the attitudes of some of the young people, providing a non-threatening environment and enabling youth workers to change lives for the better.

The Church has now grown so big that they've purchased a former British Legion building, which they've opened as a community facility and centre for worship. They have had healing services, tea dances, and are now outlining a programme of forward activities to engage with the community. I'd interview Geoff, on how they have engaged with the community over the past decade.

Tips

Remember to answer as many of the following questions as you can. You don't necessarily need *all* these things in *every* pitch, but including as many as possible, may improve your chances of success:

- What's the story?
- Why should they care?
- Why is it topical?
- Why should they assign you to write it?
- Can you provide photos?

Chapter 4
Market demand and writers' pay

Many ideological writers say you shouldn't chase the markets. "Write what you want to write", they say, and of course, it makes sense to write about your passions and exploit your expertise, but there's a balance to be struck if you're serious about making money as a writer. Meeting the requirements of commercial markets can bring in cash that enables you to spend more time writing. A newsworthy hook can add appeal too.

However, the markets are a changing phenomenon - what's 'hot' one minute, isn't necessarily 'hot' a month later. You might be able to chase the markets when working for magazines and newspapers, but what about books?

Most writers need months, if not years, to complete a book manuscript, so if your focus is on books, especially novels, then writing what you want to write, does make sense.

The question then, is what other opportunities exist for writers to increase their writing income? Beyond the obvious examples, such as writing for magazines or newspapers, have you considered whether your novel could be turned into a compelling screenplay? This sector pays well.

Best paying genres
A report on writers' pay published by the Authors' Licensing and Collecting Society in April 2016, compared what writers earned in different genres, pointing to the more profitable opportunities for

those who want to maximise their writing income.

Their survey results revealed that the highest earners were those working in audiovisual writing, such as radio and television. This is quite a specialist field, but it's accessible. Opportunities for new writers in the audiovisual sector can be found at BBC Writers' Room (www.bbc.co.uk/writersroom) and Channel 4 Talent (http://4talent.channel4.com - search screenwriting).

The second best paid genre (based on average earnings) was adult fiction, but there was considerable bias here towards higher earners. If you want to enter this market, then there are abundant opportunities for adult fiction in magazines, and a huge book market. Both are very competitive however, and there's a huge disparity between the modest earnings of the many and the high earnings of the few.

British magazines that publish adult fiction include: People's Friend, Take a Break's Fiction Feast, Woman's Weekly, Yours, My Weekly, Black Static, New Worlds, and The Edge. There are also online fiction magazines, and some in the USA and Canada that are worth a look. They include Fleeting Magazine, Flash Fiction Magazine, Washington Pastime, Cicada Magazine, Walrus, and the Boston Review.

Book publishers and agents dealing in adult fiction can be found in the Writers' and Artists' Yearbook. Some smaller publishers who deal with authors directly, include Magic Oxygen Books, John Hunt Publishing, and Skylight Press.

If you look at the median incomes (instead of mean averages), then the second best paid genre was children's fiction. See the Children's Writers' and Artists' Yearbook for agents and publishers in this genre. The children's and young adults' book market is considerable. However, British magazines in this sector tend to publish more comic strips, puzzles and crafts, than traditional short stories. Cricket Media in the USA offers opportunities for writers of children's fiction. They have a wide range of titles that carry short fiction, appealing to children of all ages (www.cricketmag.com).

After fiction, education was the next best paid genre. This sector includes writing text books, educational articles, and course materials. This is a specialist area, and you'll ideally need expertise and connections within education to make progress in this genre.

One of the lower paid genres was travel, yet it's quite an attractive genre to many aspiring writers. Opportunities in this sector include writing for airline magazines such as High Life - the British Airways magazine, Coast, National Geographic, Britain, Discover Britain, and Wanderlust. Many airlines have in-flight magazines that offer opportunities for freelancers. You don't need to travel abroad to contribute. An article about your home town might appeal to readers who are visiting the UK from overseas.

The lowest paid writers who responded to the survey were academic writers, who might typically write about their research topics. Many of them have full-time jobs at universities and writing is a small part of their working life. Their work would include contributions to specialist journals and the writing of specialist books.

Technical writing and non-fiction writing were also at the low end of the pay scale. However, without the number of hours spent writing being assigned to the survey results, it's hard to say to what extent the earnings per genre were swayed by the number of hours worked.

It's perhaps hardly surprising that those who had full-time academic positions, earned the least from their writing. They probably didn't have a lot of time to spend on writing. However, for those writers focused on the money, perhaps exploring opportunities in the most profitable genres would make some sense.

Financial rewards increase with age - to a point

The survey also showed that respondents' earnings increased with age up to the age of 50, then decreased slightly between the ages of 50 and 59, before falling sharply in retirement years.

Younger writers should perhaps feel encouraged then, that better financial rewards are yet to come. As writers develop their skills over time and grow in their role, they are able to draw on their acquired wisdom and experience to achieve higher earnings.

For older writers wondering if they've peaked, there's no need to despair. There's still a huge market for material by mature writers, in publications like The Oldie, People's Friend, Saga, The Lady, and Yours, to name just a few.

If you're wondering if you're too old to be a successful novelist think again. The author of the 'Little House on the Prairie' series of books, Laura Ingalls Wilder, didn't get a publishing deal until she was 65 years old, despite years of trying. Penelope

Fitzgerald was another author whose first book, 'The Bookshop,' wasn't published until she was 61 years old.

The gender pay gap

Is it better to be a male writer? Not necessarily. Among the 'professional authors' group, women earned 80% of what men earned, but over all, women actually earned slightly more than men when you look at all respondents combined. The gender pay gap between writers is much smaller than in other industries. So there's no real advantage to being either male or female.

Multiple incomes, related occupations, and grants

Most of the respondents had multiple income streams. Indeed, 24.81% were academics/teachers, 3.75% were retired, and over 11% defined their primary role as 'other'. Even among those who were primarily working in writing roles, such as authors, journalists, editors, and playwrights, most had another income stream. Sixty-two percent of 'authors' received over 50% of their income from other sources. There's something to be said for up-skilling and diversifying in this challenging environment.

Some writers diversify by providing photography, illustrations, or computer graphics to accompany their work. Others deliver writing workshops or do private tutoring to generate a second income. Some engage in content creation for businesses, social media management, or marketing / public relations activities.

Arts Councils provide grants for artists and writers to enable them to dedicate time to artistic works. JK Rowling received an £8000 grant from the Scottish Arts Council, before her books became hugely successful. This enabled her to work on her second Harry Potter novel, 'Harry Potter and the Chamber of Secrets', without having to worry too much about money.

Literary projects are also one of the many categories funded by the Google's Creative Work Fund (www.creativeworkfund.org).

Five ways to increase your writing income
1. Target some of the best paying sectors;
2. Draw on your expertise and experience to increase your writing income;
3. Put in long hours, work hard, and persevere;
4. Consider grants for which you're eligible;
5. Consider complementary income streams.

Who are the highest earners?
The top earners in the ALCS Writers' Pay Survey appear to be full-time writers particularly in audiovisual writing, adult fiction, and some children's fiction. However, there is wide variation between authors' earnings in every genre and there are big differences between the mean average and the median in every genre. This shows that a small number of writers are very highly paid, while the majority of writers are relatively poorly paid. However, without knowing the number of hours that the respondents spent on their writing, it's hard to be certain about just how poor their earnings were. Many were simply working part-time.

Writing success: luck, ability, or hard work?

There's always an element of luck when a writer's work gets picked up by influential people, and gains momentum in the marketplace, but a lot of a writer's success is also down hard work, talent, and a good command of written English. Dedication, commitment, and tenacity are also key attributes of successful writers.

J K Rowling wasn't an overnight success. She was a divorcee and single mother, living on benefits, who was struggling financially for years. She spent years improving her writing craft, before she found success with her Harry Potter series - which incidentally was rejected by 12 publishers before it was accepted by Bloomsbury in 1997.

Chapter 5
Writing mistakes to avoid

We're all prone to making mistakes when we start out writing. Perhaps we have clear ideas of what we want to write, genres we want to work in, and even countries we want to work for. But limiting your opportunities or markets can be a mistake. You might want to be a novelist, but don't rule out journalism or short stories. You might want to write about animals, but don't rule out capitalising on areas of expertise where you have specialist knowledge. These can be costly mistakes, that might stop you from being the best you can be, and moving forward in your writing career.

Don't limit yourself to domestic markets

Does the idea of writing for overseas markets fill you with trepidation? Don't be intimidated. Working for overseas publishers is a really good way to spread your wings and expand your portfolio.

I work for US and Australian magazines, as well as British ones, and sometimes I'm able to sell the same article to different publishers in different countries. So it's a no-brainer for anyone who's serious about making money from their writing. In fact, I find it easier to get commissions from US publishers, than from the local and regional press in my home county of Buckinghamshire! Why? Because some local editors have their favourite freelancers firmly in place, and have no appetite to work with new people that they haven't used before. Meanwhile some of the overseas editors I contact are delighted to have a fresh perspective on topics from a Brit!

So how do you get started when targeting overseas markets? Approach editors in the same way as you would in the UK. Send a polite email, containing a compelling idea and explaining why you're the best person to write the piece. Remember there are time differences, so they might respond in the middle of the night. I'm frequently communicating with my overseas clients in the evenings.

When you get paid by an overseas magazine, foreign currencies get paid into your sterling account. It's worth knowing that high street banks charge considerably less for these transactions, around £8, than some building societies.

The practicalities of trying to find out when your work is published, can be tricky, because you can't just go and browse the newsagents if the publisher is uncommunicative, but fortunately most publishers will send you a free copy when it's out.

When you start working for American and Australian magazines, you'll probably get more contracts. Their tough contracts can be quite off-putting because of the onus on the writer, and their interviewees, to pay all costs if someone sues! It's a good reason to keep your articles complimentary and harmless too. More on contracts later.

Writing for overseas markets is an interesting experience and on balance, I'd recommend it. There are many wonderful opportunities out there for determined writers. I've just sold another article to a Christian teen magazine in the USA.

Specialise

In any markets, it can be helpful if you have specialist knowledge or expertise in a subject. I'm a qualified nutritionist, so I did a lot on health and nutrition at the start of my writing career. I also worked in education for a while, so I wrote articles for teaching magazines, addressing some of the issues in that sector. One thing led to another, I took up photography, developed my skills (excuse the pun!), and ended up doing a lot of travel writing, which is a dream come true!

Whatever your specialism, writers with a good contact book, knowledge and skills, can be a valuable resource to editors. Draw on your strengths to identify suitable publications for your work. A focused, targeted approach is likely to be more successful than broad-brush strategy.

So if you're an engineer, look at what you can contribute to engineering magazines. Do you have a background in marketing? Then perhaps you can contribute to Marketing Week or Digital Marketing Magazine. Think through your specialisms and exploit them.

Know your market

Dana Huntley, the editor of British Heritage magazine in the USA says, "The old first adage of freelancing still applies: Know thy market. An editor can always tell immediately if a querying writer is familiar with the magazine they're trying to pitch."

If they're not, "that's doomed" he says. "Every story needs to be targeted for a specific publication and its readership. Know the difference between a topic and a story. Unless you're Bill Bryson, no editor is going to just let an author write 'about' something. A query, like an essay, must have a thesis."

Many editors want stories that are topical, or have a 'hook', making the ideas relevant to the magazine's audience on the date when they publish. There often needs to be a compelling reason to run the story.

Dana adds, "Never suggest to an editor that you know, better than they do, what would be good for their readers." Comments such as 'I know your readers would love this', or 'This would be terrific for your magazine', are not always welcome."

Mind your spelling! Mind your grammar!

Always make sure your query email has flawless grammar and spelling. An editor can tell a lot about a writers' skill set and style from their first email.

One editor told me that I needed to read up on the difference between 'which' and 'that' in my writing. This was hugely embarrassing. I was an established writer who'd been getting it wrong for years! I dived into grammar books the same day, and had lengthy discussions with my husband on the subject.

It seemed odd that no-one had mentioned it before, but I eventually concluded that this was because few people seem to be aware of the rules. The explanations in grammar books might make your head explode, and I've read whole books where authors get it wrong throughout. Frankly, a lot of people ignore the rules. But as writers, we should always strive to do better.

So the moral of my story is to get really hot on your grammar if you want to be a professional writer. It's embarrassing and makes you look unprofessional when an editor feels they have to correct you. As writers we should be experts on this stuff.

Also, if you're approaching US or Australian markets, adjust your spelling to show you can write in American English. Also remember they use different words for certain things - like 'zucchinis' for courgettes, and 'pants' for trousers. It's important to become familiar with US English as best you can, so you minimise the editing required by the publisher, and they'll want to use you again.

Check your facts!
When researching historical documents, you'll often find different sources give conflicting dates for key events. You need to be able to justify the reliability of your facts in these circumstances. Also, sometimes editors will ask questions about things that you haven't even considered! So it's helpful to have done your research, and know where to find the answer, even if you don't know it off hand. Fill your article with interesting details and be ready to answer any queries that come up. Train yourself to think beyond the obvious and have an inquisitive mind.

Diane Wordsworth, a prolific writer of magazine articles and books, says, "One of my best sales was my first overseas sale, to Spa Magazine in America. It earned me £1,850, plus three very nice days out at a spa. I got meals and my travel expenses paid too! They checked and checked and checked every fact - Every Single Fact. I hadn't realised they would be so particular. I don't know if that's just how they do things over there. I wasn't expecting so many hour-long phone calls, but it opened my eyes. They didn't even find anything wrong with my copy after all that fact checking!"

Understand the readership

Simon Whaley, the author of four writing books and numerous magazine articles says, "Identifying the core readership of a foreign publication isn't always easy, because it's difficult to analyse the market in the same detail as you can with a home-grown publication. This means it's easier to make mistakes.

"I once pitched an idea to an American travel publication about the UK's Lake District, with the specific angle of telling them about some of its lesser-known lakes. I came up with a top ten, suggesting a piece about why they should be visited and how to get there.

"The editor said he liked the idea, but his readership were not the type to trek a mile across open hillside to visit a lake. Nor were they inclined to drive along some of the narrow, single-track roads we have in the Lake District.

"So although I'd pitched the right topic, and an interesting idea, the mistake I'd made was not tailoring it to the readership. Of course, I reworked my pitch, and identified seven lakes that were still relatively uncommon, but easily accessible. The editor bought this, which proves that it doesn't matter if you make a mistake, as long as you learn from it!"

Chapter 6
Finding new homes for articles that get rejected

There's no doubt about it: publishing can be a very tough business. I've had articles accepted and then later rejected, following editorial changes. Articles commissioned and accepted by one editor, were subsequently rejected without pay by his successor. This is demoralising, as you can imagine. But it is possible to rehome articles in these circumstances. Sometimes they just need tweaking to make them suitable for new markets.

I ended up making more money from some of these articles than I would have done if the original editor had published them in the first place. That's a nice feeling.

1) The first article I rehomed was an article on an unusual museum. It was rejected by the editor of a nostalgia publication, so I sold it to a regional lifestyle magazine in Cornwall, who paid me 50% more than the magazine who'd changed their mind.

2) A rejected article on the history and revival of Rollerama, was sold to a Scottish magazine with some minor amendments to make it more 'Scottish'. My local rag also ran a short column on the topic. So I got two new sales from that rejection.

3) A magazine who commissioned a piece on my family history first accepted, and then rejected it, so I rehomed the piece with another publication who

paid on acceptance.

4) An article on animal therapy was commissioned by a pet magazine, and then rejected a year later because their editorial needs had changed. It was rehomed with a general interest magazine who paid and ran the piece very quickly.

5) An article on life in Victorian workhouses was revised to include details of former workhouses in Scotland and sold to a Scottish regional magazine. It was also reworked for a US magazine interested in the topic. In the end I got two new sales from that rejection, and accrued considerably more money from the extra effort put in, than I would have received if the original magazine had published it as planned.

6) An article on Doctor Who film locations was rejected, and rejigged for a countryside magazine, who paid more for the article than I would have received from the original commission.

7) An article about a former Wren was rejected by a military magazine, who commissioned it and then scrapped the column for which it was intended. I sold the article to a regional magazine in Sussex instead - that's where the Wren lived. The military magazine has since come back and now wants to run the story!

8) An article that was rejected by one of my business clients, because I'd misunderstood the brief, was rejigged and sold to a regional magazine for their

health pages.

So you can see there's plenty of scope for rehoming articles, even if they don't get accepted by the publisher who commissioned the work. When you're doing a lot of freelance wrirting, there are bound to be some articles that fall by the wayside, but the key is to keep your wits about you, and constantly analyse the markets, so you're aware of opportunities to rehome any articles that hit the 'reject' pile.

Chapter 7
Understanding rights

When you get a commission from a publisher, whether it's a newspaper, magazine, or a book publisher, you might be faced with a complicated legal contract demanding certain rights. The legal jargon can feel overwhelming, but don't dismay. A lot of it is standard and it's designed to ensure that you both know your legal positions and obligations under the terms of the agreement.

Your creative work, such as writing and photography, is automatically covered by copyright as soon you as you create it. So when a publisher wants to publish your work, they are buying a the 'rights' (usually a license) to print it. It's a good idea to be clear on which rights are expected, firstly to protect your own interests, secondly to ensure you understand what opportunities exist for re-sales, and finally because any misunderstanding or confusion about which rights you've assigned to your publisher, may compromise your position legally.

First Rights
Most publishers are primarily interested in first rights. This means they buy the rights to publish your work before anyone else. They might want First British Rights, First North American Rights, or First World Rights. If you sell First British Rights in the UK, you can still sell First North American Rights to a US publisher, or First Australian Rights to an Australian publisher, and so on.

Reprints / Second Rights

Once you've sold first rights, you can still sell reprints (sometimes called second rights) to another publisher. For example, I've sold war memoirs, originally written for a military history magazine, to general interest publications as reprints. You can sell reprints as many times as you like. Publications willing to consider reprints are often small presses, with tiny budgets, but don't be put off by the low pay - if you can make an extra £20 to £50 for a straight reprint, why not?

World Rights

There is a growing demand for world rights, because publishers want to be able to post your work on their websites. You may wonder then, how this affects your potential for overseas sales? Well, it could affect them considerably, but that depends somewhat on your subject matter and to what extent it would need to be adapted for sale to an overseas publication anyway. When your article appears online, it means world rights have been sold (or assumed), and this makes your article less attractive to overseas publishers.

However, working for overseas markets often requires considerable reworking of an article. Different countries have different uses of language and may require a lot of adaptation, taking into account cultural sensitivities, climate considerations, relevance to audience, and subtle differences in the meaning of language.

When I reworked a British health article for the Australian market, I took into account language differences (spellings and foods that have different names), climate differences (fresh foods that people can typically grow in Australia) and sourced Australian studies and research materials, making the topic totally relevant to Australian readers. I also had to adapt my work to the style of the publication, with more box outs. By the time I'd done all that, it was a quite different article.

The original article had appeared in a British publication, citing UK and US studies, quoting foods that grow well in the UK, and using British spellings and etiquette. They were similar, but different.

The extent to which any article will cross borders without extra work, varies enormously, and so do editorial policies. Some editors won't touch an article that has previously appeared online. But others might not be concerned, especially if it's only appeared on a foreign website that their readers probably haven't seen. It's worth querying opportunities in overseas countries if you think there's a reasonable chance of a sale, even if your article has appeared on a British website. Just be honest about it.

All Rights or Copyright
Some publishers are now demanding 'all rights' or copyright of your work, so that they can feel completely free to do as they please with it. Some experts say that technically, the sale of 'all rights' usually still leaves you with copyright ownership, but because you've sold all rights, you cannot sell or license your work to anyone else. Some publishers distinguish between the two. However, in practise, the sale of all rights has the same impact on your future income, as the sale of copyright. Some

publishers may say their all rights contract includes the sale of copyright. Many writers resist selling all rights, as it means they cannot generate any future income from that particular piece of work.

In the USA, editorial demands for all rights are becoming increasingly common, for both words and pictures. To be clear, once you have sold these rights, you can't use your own article or photos in a self-published anthology, or on your blog. You would need to buy a license to do so from the publisher who purchased your work.

This might make all rights contracts seem unattractive, but some publishers won't compromise. Worse, they might send you an all rights contract, *after* you've done the work. That happened to me once when an existing client was in the process of changing their contracts. So it's worth checking the rights required by a publisher *before* accepting a commission. It's also worth taking lots of photos to accompany your articles in case you're required to sell copyright to some of those pictures.

Simon Whaley, the author of 'The Complete Article Writer', 'Photography for Writers', and 'The Positively Productive Writer', says, "I avoid all rights contracts where possible, because you can't do anything else with your work. However, it depends upon the job. Non-fiction is easier to rewrite than fiction. If a publisher takes all rights in a 500-word walking route description, it's just those 500 words they're taking all rights in, not the actual walk itself. There's nothing stopping me rewriting the walk description in 1,000 words, or more. But I've stopped submitting fiction to markets that ask for all rights, because I can't submit that story to other markets around the world, or include it in one of my self-published short story eBook collections."

The authors of the Writer's Digest 'Handbook of Magazine Article Writing' suggest that writers faced with all rights contracts should try to negotiate. "Find common ground," they advise, "If a publication wants all rights, see where the wiggle room lies. Will the editor settle for exclusive rights for a certain time period, after which she can retain a non-exclusive license to the content? It remains your property, but the publication can use it. Or maybe the editor will settle for the rights in a specific subject area, like competing publications. This way, if you find a publication with no competing interests, you can resell the work."

Other rights

Other rights that publishers may ask for include anthology rights; book rights; electronic rights for e-publications, or internet rights for publishing on the world wide web - that is always a world right. This is not exhaustive, but gives you a feel for the kinds of rights you might be asked for and what they mean. Editorial contracts will usually explain in greater detail exactly what is required anyway. If you don't understand a contract, always ask for clarification. The legal jargon can be a bit cumbersome and you need to ensure you understand what you're being asked to sign.

British publishers and overseas markets

A lot of British magazines and niche newspapers don't issue contracts at all. In the absence of a contract, the default position is that they usually want First British Serial Rights - a license to print your article in the UK before it is offered for publication elsewhere. They may also require a license to print your pictures, whether they've been previously published or not. The 'Serial' bit relates to a serial publication - a magazine that is published regularly for example, as opposed to a book, which might be a one off.

If a magazine or newspaper wants to publish your work on their website too, they may ask for world rights. However in my experience, they're more likely to just assume that's OK. The first you'll know about it is when you 'Google' your name and your article pops up on your clients' website! As far as I'm concerned, that's fine. Goodwill between writer and editor is far more important to most writers, than whether or not the publisher pays a surplus to put a printed article on their website too.

When you sell to overseas publishers, demands for all rights on photography may be more of a sticking point than requests for all rights on the words. Words can be rehashed, while getting new photos might require considerable time, cost and travel. Take plenty of photographs when you're on location so that you can sell some outright if you need to. Then you'll still have enough left to illustrate other articles in the future.

It also makes sense to maximise the opportunities for sales and licensing outside the USA before approaching American publishers who are more likely to demand all rights to everything.

Finally, remember to file your contracts in a place where you can find them. Then, if you have any doubts about what rights you've sold to a publisher, you can look it up and consider whether there are opportunities to sell your work into other paying markets as reprints, rewrites/adaptations, or as overseas sales.

Chapter 8
Understanding contracts

As a writer, making sure you understand the complex language of legal contracts is important. If you don't understand the terms, you might overlook small but significant details that could compromise your future income. These details can make the difference between being able to exploit opportunities and generate a good income from your work, and running the risk of not being properly remunerated for your work.

Publishers in the USA are big on contracts. I've never received work from a US publisher without having to sign a contract first. So what kinds of terms can you expect to see?

- Contracts demanding the transfer of copyright from writer to publisher are not uncommon, although most publishers will pay reasonably well for this privilege.

- Contracts putting all the legal risks back onto the writer are very common in the USA.

- Contracts with an opt-out clause, relinquishing the publisher from any obligation to actually publish, or pay for, what they've assigned you to write.

- Some contracts forbid you from selling a similar article to competing publications.

- Some contracts give the publisher the right to sub-licence your work to third parties. You may, or may not, get a fee for these sales.

- Some contracts demand that your work is placed into the public domain under a Creative Commons licence. This means you give up copyright, so that

45

anyone can use it.

Understanding contracts is important for any writer. They affect your pay, your potential for future sales, your right to pitch to competing publications, your right to use the work on another platform (perhaps on your blog or in a book), and your legal position in different scenarios. As a writer, you'll want to comply with your contractual obligations and stay out of legal hot water. Also, understanding whether a contract is offering a good deal financially or not, can make the difference between being able to write for a living, and being a frustrated hobbyist.

Social or community journalism

One area where you need to read the contracts with care is in the emerging world of social or community journalism. It's gaining a lot of attention at the moment, because it enables anyone to try their hand at being a news reporter, and gives unpublished writers a quick route to publication. Platforms include Gawker, Buzzfeed, and Blasting News.

It's wise to read the contract or T&Cs when you 'join' a social journalism community, or any other kind of third-party publishing platform. The terms of use vary, and may place restrictions on how else you can use any work you upload to the site. At least one such platform makes all their contributors agree to a 'Copyright Transfer Agreement', which hands over copyright to the publisher. This means the publisher owns the exclusive right to print, publish, and reproduce anything posted on the site by contributors. So you can't then exploit your work in any other way.

Social journalism sites tend to have a mix of paid

and unpaid contributors. Some have different submission requirements for paid contributors, compared to their unpaid counterparts. Paid contributors may earn a modest fee in return for meeting minimum requirements, such as attracting 150+ unique visitors to their news item. There's potential to earn greater sums if your post goes viral.

Some platforms, such as Forbes.com, pay their regular 'hand picked' contributors according to a pre-arranged number of posts and specified level of audience engagement in terms of reader comments.

On at least one platform, if the publisher deletes your work from their website, you can't use it for anything else, because they still own the copyright. Termination of the agreement does not affect the transfer of rights.

It's quite common for publishers, especially those based in the US, to assign responsibility for any legal claims or disputes regarding your work, back to the writer. You're not protected against legal action, so caution is required, as in most areas of writing.

Social journalism does provide an unpublished writer with the opportunity to be published, and perhaps paid, so it's certainly not all bad news, but you just need to go into it with your eyes open.

Traditional journalism
In more traditional newspaper or magazine journalism, most contracts still enable writers to exploit the full potential of their work, only asking for first rights to print your work, or reprints. However, requests for copyright are becoming more common, so it pays to read every contract carefully and make sure that you fully understand what you're

signing.

Also be aware of contracts that state you cannot write anything similar for another publication. This clause rules out rewrites and reworked articles on the same topic - anything that might be deemed 'similar'. It may not be a problem, but you still need to be aware of your obligations.

The publisher of my first book, *Freelance Writing on Health, Food and Gardens*, had a clause in their contract, saying ebook conversion costs came out of royalties. This was something I'd completely missed. The top of the contract clearly stated that the author contribution was 'zero', which seemed contradictory to this clause. So I challenged the clause, and to my surprise, they didn't deduct the royalties, but you can't rely on that. If there's something you don't agree with in a contract, you need to challenge it before signing the contract, not afterwards when the penny drops!

Now if all that legal jargon sends your head into a spin, there are people out there who can help. The Society of Authors has a service where they will check your book contracts and give you helpful feedback. While technically, this service is for members who have received book contracts, I've heard of authors who've also asked them to look at other types of publishing contracts, such as magazine contracts. I understand they're very helpful. The Society of Authors can flag up some useful points and areas for negotiation if a contract seems unreasonable. This is part of the membership package, so it's worth considering joining the Society of Authors if contracts and legal jargon seem like a foreign language to you.

Sometimes contracts are negotiable, although often they're not. I did have words with the editor of a US magazine who issued a new contract demanding copyright on photographs, *after* I'd done the work. Their eventual climb-down on this issue was probably down to a number of complaints from many of their writers. I'd be surprised if my email alone, had such a dramatic effect.

Usually contracts offered by publishers are not negotiable. But if you're really unhappy with the terms, it's worth trying to find a compromise. You might be pleasantly surprised. I've found that my latest contract from a commercial book publisher is actually remarkably flexible.

Here are some of the terms in contracts I've received over the years:

"You assign, transfer and make over to IPC Media Limited absolutely the entirety of your right, title and interest in and to the copyright and all other rights of every kind or description now or hereafter..."
Amateur Gardening magazine, UK.

The author gives the publisher the *"non-exclusive right for the DCT Group to syndicate your contribution subject to payment to you of 50% of all net revenues received by DCT Group and attributable to such contribution."*
DC Thomson, UK.

"Any article submitted must not have been published elsewhere and, if published by us, becomes exclusive to Yours magazine on an all-rights basis."
Yours magazine, UK.

"This agreement can be terminated with 24 hours notice without any charge."
NFU Countryside magazine, UK.

"In no event shall said material be published in any competing domestic publication." Beckett Media, USA.

"Author shall indemnify and hold Publisher harmless from and against any and all third party claims, losses, liabilities, damages, expenses and costs, including, without limitation, reasonable fees for attorneys, expert witnesses and litigation costs..."
Rock and Gem magazine, USA.

"All copyright and trademark interests therein, shall be deemed to belong solely and exclusively to the publisher, and the freelancer shall not have any interest therein"
Kliger Heritage Media LLC, USA.

I can't stress enough how important it is to read the contract in full and ensure you understand what you're signing. Failure to do this could leave you at the wrong end of a law suit. Also, on a practical level, you can't negotiate better terms if you don't read and understand the contract.

Chapter 9
Taking your blog from obscurity to success

British writer, Ruth Holroyd, is the brains behind the award-winning blog www.whatallergy.com. She started blogging about places to eat for people with multiple allergies, and the blog became so successful, it's now expanded to include her experiences with allergies, eczema, and to discuss a wide variety of allergy-related topics.

"I have severe multiple allergies, including nuts, dairy, soya, wheat, latex, nickel and dust," she says,

"I've just discovered that I'm now allergic to chestnuts too - I collect new allergies every day!

"I began blogging in 2009, and my followers, many of whom suffer from severe allergies too, now top 120,000 unique visitors every month. My blog won the Free-From Food Award in November 2014, and was named by Cision UK as one of the top five allergy blogs, and top ten health blogs, for two years running.

"As the blog's following grew, companies started contacting me, asking to advertise on my blog. I do accept advertising that is relevant to people with allergies, but decline non-relevant products, such as online gambling sites. I also participate in affiliate schemes from www.clickbank.com on allergy-related topics. When someone clicks through and buys from an affiliate, I get a commission."

The combination of relevant advertising, affiliates, and sponsored articles, enables Ruth to earn about £400 a month from her blog, which she writes in her spare time. Her day job is working as a self-employed copywriter and marketing professional. She is constantly immersed in the world of allergies and related topics because she works with 'free from' food industry clients, writing copy, attending shows and taking part in exhibitions.

With so much going on in her working life, you'd think Ruth might struggle to find the time to write blogs on the side, but the blog is important to her. She says, "I write to share stuff I've learnt, to help others, and as a therapy; the latter being very high on the list. Writing about having allergies and ranting occasionally about things that get me irate helps me to process this condition and develop coping mechanisms. I write a journal too which is invaluable when struggling with difficult decisions."

Ruth's blog looks at all sorts of allergy-related topics including eczema, asthma, 'free from' foods, eating out, alternative remedies, coeliac disease, EU regulations, cosmetics, disabilities and sensitive skin, to name just a few.

"I post a new blog once every week," she says and when I ask her if there's any conflict between the commercial interests of her daytime work and the health-promoting vision of her blog, she surprises me, with an unabashed, "Yes!"

Ruth explains, "I get sent stuff by a variety of companies and recently received some gluten-free cornflakes and honey flakes. They're gluten-free but they're not healthy. Many of the products I get sent cause horrible allergic reactions that make me sick. They're full of all sorts of additives and other nasty ingredients. I'm not huge fan of processed foods. Free-from shopping is supposed to be healthy, but many of the products aren't healthy at all.

"I try to follow the principle of eating products that have five ingredients or fewer. My grandma used to say, 'If you don't know what it is, don't eat it'. That sounded like good advice to me and I've tried to follow it, by avoiding strangely named additives like Butylated hydroxytoluene.

"I limit the products on my blog to those that I like. I don't want to recommend foods that are unhealthy, or cosmetics that might bring people out in a rash! This makes me unpopular with some people who think I'm too strict.

"Some foods I was sent recently were really sweet and give me a head rush - I refuse to write about those kinds of products and send them back. I write about natural skin care stuff too, and there's one well-known brand that's keen to be featured on my blog, but their soap gives me blisters, so I won't be featuring it.

"I'm about to start writing about a new brand of tea that to date, has not been widely available in the UK. I also get paid to write about some Holland and Barrett products; Nairns oat cakes, which I like; and Tangled Teaser - a weird brush that's really soft and good for getting tangles out of your hair.

"I work for the Free From Food Awards and get paid to write restaurant reviews. I'm also on the judging panel for the Free From Skin Care Awards, which is an interesting experience! I'm speaking at the Allergy Show in July, although that one's a freebee. Fortunately, I do get paid to promote a propolis solution for sold sores. The product's really good and I'm happy to recommend it.

"I was interviewed on Radio 5 Live when the new allergy regulations came into force last year, forcing restaurants to cater for people with allergies. One-hundred chefs banded together arguing that the regulations would ruin their creativity. I saw things differently and blogged about it. Radio 5 saw my blog and invited me onto the show to present my argument from the perspective of someone who can't eat out because they have allergies.

"Then the BBC news team came to my house wanting to know how the regulations would affect me. I've reviewed allergy books on my blog and I've got a cookery book called Cooking Allergy Free to review at the moment. I write 'Ruth's Allergy Diary', a blog for the Food Matters website, and I manage their Twitter account. I write case studies on adrenaline injection pens that generates an income too. When I'm not doing all that, I do exhibition work for Anytime Fitness!"

Tell me about the interaction on your blog

"Generally the interaction is really positive and people are so pleased that I'm able to understand their challenges and help them a bit. There's very little conflict, although one blog I wrote on the use of perfumes generated some conflict! I enjoy constructive disagreements and debates.

"I've written a few blogs about how I think people should stop moaning and just get on with life. I know it's crap to have allergies, but you have to get over the 'suffering' mentality, or you'll be suffering for the rest of your life.

"There are alternative foods available and there are always people worse off than you. You may not be able to eat cake, but you can probably eat an apple. People don't like to hear that, but I want to change the way people think, so that they're not always feeling like a 'sufferer'.

"Ninety-nine percent of people don't die from an anaphylactic reaction. It's a horrible thing to happen to you, but statistically you're more likely to be murdered than to die from an anaphylactic reaction.

"I feel that it's necessary for people with allergies to move away from the suffering mentality because otherwise they're constantly moaning and people will stop wanting to socialise with them. I take a 'shut up and pull your socks up' approach, which reflects my upbringing."

Is it rewarding to know that you're helping people?

"Oh yes! I find writing a blog so rewarding. I don't do it to make money. It's more about helping people than anything else. Even though I've never met most of my followers, I feel like I know some of them because they're so grateful. People e-mail me with questions and I'm e-mailing people every week to point them in the right direction - to charities that can help them for example. I'm a second point of contact when their doctors turn around and say they can't help. There are all sorts of charities that can help that doctors don't tell you about.

"I'm not a medical practitioner, so I always include a disclaimer, telling people to check with their doctor before trying anything new. My blog is all about my personal experiences and about products that people might find helpful - I don't offer health advice on my blog or in emails, because as I'm not qualified to do that."

What have been your greatest website challenges and are there any hidden costs?

"My brother built my website and I pay £100 for a web-maintenance professional to do a couple of hours work, updating spam filters, and keeping it safe because hackers are trying to access it all the time. I have 500 spam messages go into the spam filter every month. Fortunately I don't see them because he deals with all this for me. Apart from that, I just Google how to do things on WordPress and manage to do most things myself. The main costs are the costs of the URL and website hosting.

"The blog is very time consuming and can be quite wearing. It takes ages to respond to all the e-mail enquiries. I don't have enough time to do everything myself, so it's helpful to have some help.

"At one time, my website hosts kept shutting my blog down because it was generating too much traffic and slowing down their servers, so I had to change to a different website host. Wordpress itself was fine - it's the website hosting company who owns the server that was causing the problem.

"I do stuff for charities that incurs costs too, but I'm glad to do that because I think it makes me a better person. When I'm not helping people, I feel less motivated. I love it.

"Sometimes I write what I think is a great blog and it gets no comments. Other blogs get loads of comments. As bloggers, we have a lot of power and a bad product review can be really damaging. I don't write bad reviews, but it's a nice position to be in."

What tips would you give to people who want to draw traffic to their own blog?

"Social media is really important for sharing stuff, but it's not a one-way street. You need to comment on what other people share and link up with other bloggers. I've got loads of blogs that I follow and there's an etiquette to link back if someone else's work has inspired your blog.

"It makes sense to spend time learning what makes a good blog. They shouldn't be too long. Five-hundred to 1000 words is a maximum length. You do learn what works from experience. People thought I'd get bored doing this when I started, but I don't. I always have something I want to say on the topic as it affects my life so much.

"Some blogs I write quickly, others take years of

testing products, finding links, and perfecting the wording. It can be a hard slog."

How do you progress to running adverts and affiliate links down the side?

"It's fairly simple. I just put an image with a link down the side. There are more effective ways of getting your product noticed though. People gloss over advertising a lot these days. A sponsored blog post or product review is a better approach.

"You need to get good hit rates for advertising to work, or you won't make much money from it. I'm an Amazon affiliate, but I don't make much from that."

What advice would you give to someone who wanted to make money from their blog?

People use blogs because they like an independent voice. So be careful you don't have adverts everywhere. Make it subtle. I use Google Adsense as well as putting my own links up. I link back to blogs I like - reciprocal links can work two ways, supporting other bloggers and drawing traffic to your blog too.

"Add your blog to your e-mail signature. Don't rely on friends and family to be your biggest supporters. My friends are too busy to look most of the time. It's the people who have allergies and benefit from my blogs that show the most commitment to the blog and comment on my posts.

"My followers live all over the world and they all seem to think that I'm from their home country. I get comments from people living in the Philippines, Australia and China. Sometimes that complain that they can't get products where they live, and unfollow me!"

How does a blogger grow from obscurity to success?

"Write about something you care about, and something that isn't being done already. If you haven't got a passion you can run out of steam very quickly. You also need to have reasonable writing skills so that you come across well and your blog isn't full of mistakes.

"I learn from my blog's statistics. You can see what people are interested in. Keep an eye on what works well and what doesn't. I write more of the things that people value. I write four or five blogs at a time and then schedule them.

"I'd also recommend carrying a notebook to jot down ideas. I currently have 99 drafts of things I'm working on! Google likes things that change a lot and your SEO words need to be relevant. There's a lot you can read about blogging on the Internet if you want to learn more. It's always worth looking at Twitter for blogging events. Search on 'blogging' or 'blog meet ups' and go to ones that interest you. You'll learn a lot about blogging at these events."

Chapter 10
Website Content Creation

One way to get work as a writer is to target websites looking for content. The pay varies enormously, but there's always a need for new content, and considerable opportunity for those interested in this area of work.

Every commercial website needs new and regularly updated copy to keep their visitors interested and encourage people to keep returning to the site. Brian A. Klems from Writer's Digest says, "countless corporations, nonprofits and even small companies are turning to web-savvy writers as they look to appeal to consumers through blog posts, articles and other content supplementing their products and services."

So how do you access these markets? I've targeted some websites directly by writing in and asking who to pitch my ideas to. It's led to regular work. There are many different approaches however; some people like to browse freelance writing job sites for a mix of freelance and staff opportunities. I've used www.thecontentcloud.net before and find that site quite useful. Other opportunities can be found on the following sites:

www.elance.com
www.gorkanajobs.com
www.upwork.com
www.mediabistro.com
www.journalismjobs.com
www.online-writing-jobs.com
www.freelancewritinggigs.com

www.writers-editors.com

Pay is variable, but choose carefully and there are some gems to be had. Regular clients can come from these jobs.

Some sites designed for freelancers require subscriptions to be paid. However, this sorts the serious writers from those just passing through, and reduces the level of competition. www.freelancesuccess.com is considered to be among the better ones, offering a market guide and an online networking community that you may find valuable.

Join social media groups for writers to make contacts. You might meet interesting people, including business or editorial contacts. I've met quite a few people on social media who have subsequently featured in my articles. I've also heard about new publishing opportunities, one of which led to a book deal.

Get out to industry events and make business connections too. Business networking groups might be a good place to start if you want to write for local businesses, but don't restrict yourself geographically - there's no reason why you can't approach companies overseas if you have the specialist knowledge and skills that they might be looking for in a writer.

Many businesses want a strong social media presence, but don't have time to do it themselves. You can run their social media accounts for them, and write their blogs. This is a thriving area. It blends writing with marketing and it's a way of generating more income as a professional writer.

Chapter 11
How to self-publish for free

Many writers have a passion for books, and while writing articles or short stories is a great way to earn money from your writing, it may not fulfill that deeply seated desire to see your book in print.

The great news is that the world of publishing is evolving and the traditional route of having to find an agent, then a publisher, and wait at least a year for publication of your book, is no longer considered essential for success.

The emergence of self-publishing tools like Kindle and Createspace have made it easy for anyone to publish their own work free of charge, and sell it through the world's biggest bookstore, Amazon (and their extended distribution network).

If you prefer to publish through another platform, such as Smashwords, FeedaRead, Lulu, Ingram Sparks, or Lightning Source, take your pick! There are many low- or zero-cost options available.

Self-publishing is now so easy, fast, efficient, cost-effective and lucrative, that many authors are choosing to self-publish in preference to going the traditional route. Why? Speed, convenience, control, and cold hard cash. Authors tend to receive better royalties per sale from self-publishing than from traditional book deals, so the DIY model can be quite appealing. However, the self-publishing approach does put all the onus on the author to get out there and sell their books. This doesn't suit everyone. Traditional publishers may have more resources in terms of marketing and sales teams, and access to high street stores. These assets can boost sales considerably, making up for low royalties per sale, and boosting your author profile. However, not all traditional publishers have a lot of resources, so it's worth doing your homework. Traditional publishers also expect authors to be proactive and help with the marketing, so you usually have to step up and get involved, whichever route you take.

How to publish on Createspace

Amazon's Createspace enables you to publish a paperback book on Amazon, and through other sales channels if you wish. There is no catch. They simply take a commission on any sales you make, and pay out any royalties you're due. It's easy to upload your manuscript, and the step by step instructions enable anyone to become a published author, without any financial outlay.

- Go to: www.createspace.com
- Press the blue 'Sign Up' button on the left of the screen.
- A form will appear. Type in your details, and when it asks, 'What type of media are you considering publishing?' choose 'Book'.
- Make a record of your password so you can access your account in future.
- When you've filled everything in, press 'Create My Account'.
- You will then be taken to the terms and conditions. Read, agree, and continue.
- You have to verify your email address. Then a link in the email will take you to a page where you can start creating your book.

- The 'name of your project' is your book title. Choose 'Paperback', and select the 'Guided Set Up' process.
- Fill in your name under Primary Author. Ignore 'Add Contributors', unless there's another author involved in your project.
- You can skip the rest if you wish. Just press 'Save and Continue'.
- Choose 'Free CreateSpace-Assigned ISBN'. Click 'Assign Free ISBN' and then press 'Continue'.
- Black ink on white paper is the default setting, so you don't need to change anything, unless you want to publish in colour, which would increase the purchase price of your book considerably.
- You do need to choose the size of your book. Createspace recommends 6"x9". Underneath the 'Choose a different size' heading, is a link to a template. Once you've chosen the size of your book, click on 'blank template'. This will open a word document in the correct dimensions. Just copy and paste your manuscript straight into it.
- Now check through your book. Do the headings appear where you want them? Do the page breaks appear where you want them? Do you want page numbers and a contents page? Make changes to the document until you are satisfied with it, and save it somewhere that you can find it later.
- Once you're happy with your book's interior, scroll down in Createspace, and upload your book file, by clicking, 'browse'. Select your book.
- If you've logged out, log back into Createspace and click on your book title. Then click on the

interior page, and you can upload the file.

- It takes a little while for your book to go through Createspace's 'Automated Print Check', so be patient. When this process is complete, press 'Launch Interior Reviewer', press 'Get Started', and use the arrows to scroll through the book, checking that it looks good inside. If you're happy with the interior, press 'Save and Continue'.

- If you're not happy, you can amend the original Word document, and upload the new document onto Createspace, replacing the old one. Just repeat the process until you're satisfied.

- When you're happy with the book's interior, press 'Continue'. If you change your mind, you can go back and change it at any time.

- Now move onto the cover design. Choose a matte or glossy cover. Click 'Build your Cover Online'. Then 'Launch Cover Creator'.

- When a screen of book covers appears, double-click on a cover image that you like. You can change the words on your book cover by clicking on the links on the left and typing in new text. Click on any part of the book image to open the edit box on the left.

- Once you are happy with your book cover, press 'Submit Cover'. If you have any problems, or prefer to upload your own cover, you can save your own cover as a PDF, ensuring it meets the size specifications for your book, and 'Submit'.

- With your cover submitted, press 'Continue'. Then, if you're happy with everything on the final summary page, press 'Submit files for

Review'. This sends your book to Createspace to check.

- They will inform you by email if anything needs fixing. Otherwise, within 24 hours, you should have a proof waiting for you to view online. You can order a hard copy proof if you wish. They are shipped from the USA so proofs are expensive. If you are reasonably sure that your book is OK, it's actually cheaper to publish it on Amazon, and buy a copy from Amazon in the UK.

- Before you publish, you will be asked to set a price, add a description, set keywords, and select distribution channels. It's very straight forward. If you haven't done so already, you will also need to add bank details under 'Account Settings' so they can pay you royalties on your sales.

- When your book has been approved, and you're happy with the final proof, press 'Publish' in Createspace, and it will appear on Amazon, usually within 24 hours. Orders are printed on demand and delivered quickly by Royal Mail.

- You can still go back into your book, and make changes at any time.

How to publish on Kindle

Createspace creates a Kindle file and will automatically upload it onto Kindle Direct Publishing if you select 'Publish on Kindle', under the 'Distribute' menu. This is a simple process. You sign into Kindle Direct Publishing with your Amazon account, or create an account here: www.amazonkdp.com. The step by step instructions are easy to follow. Createspace has done most of it for you. Just add a few more details, set the price, and publish. Allow 24 hours for it to appear on Amazon.

Pros and Cons

Preparing the book files can be time-consuming and fiddly, but in my opinion, it's worth it. Createspace offers a fast, efficient way of getting your book into print, and it's free!

Case study

Dave Sivers had a manuscript kicking around his house for ten years before he published on Amazon Kindle in 2011. He's since published five more ebooks through Kindle Direct Publishing, three paperbacks through Createspace, and has sold over 15,000 copies in total! His newest title, a crime thriller called 'Evil Unseen', was published in January 2016.

Chapter 12
Generating book reviews

So you've written the next bestseller, self-published on Amazon, tweeted about it until all your followers are bored, and sold a few to your friends. Now you wait. You've sold dozens, but the book, despite being a work of complete genius, has no reviews. How will potential buyers know how good it is, unless someone writes a review? Your friends are very complimentary about it, but don't get round to reviewing. It's frustrating. Then you stumble across someone offering a review for a fiver? Worthwhile? Perhaps not.

In October 2015 Amazon started legal action against over 1,000 unidentified people who it claims, wrote fake reviews on www.Amazon.com in return for a fee. Many such reviewers were advertising their services through a website called 'Fiver', offering reviews in return for $5 (about £4).

In early October, The Sunday Times investigated the practice, with journalists paying reviewers £56 to give their new ebook, 'Everything Bonsai!', a five-star rating. This book, which was riddled with errors and written over a weekend, made it to the top of Amazon UK's Kindle category for gardening and horticulture.

The Competition and Markets Authority in the UK reported that 54% of UK adults read online reviews, and use them to make purchasing decisions. However, fake reviews are starting to undermine consumer confidence.

So where does this leave authors seeking genuine

reviews of their works?

Standing out from the crowd, differentiating yourself, and persuading readers to give your book a chance, is every new author's challenge. But don't be lured into *buying* five star reviews. Genuine feedback is infinitely more beneficial to both the author and their readers, who incidentally, are becoming more savvy. Short and shallow reviews, offering no insight into the content of the book, will be unlikely to make much difference to sales figures.

Genuine book reviews however, are important to help generate sales and build an author's brand. They give readers an independent perspective on your work, and can help you, as a writer, develop your writing skills. Even disappointing reviews can help a writer to hone their craft. It's just one person's opinion. Think about whether the feedback can be used to make your next book even better, and then move on and focus on the positive feedback you've received.

Fortunately for writers, most people only review books they've enjoyed, so there's usually a favourable balance. Positive feedback can build confidence that you're getting it right, and a mixture of feedback just shows that your reviews are real - because nobody's work will appeal to everyone.

To generate more reviews, many authors are now ending their books with the message, "If you enjoyed this book, please consider leaving a review". According to some self-publishing gurus, such as David Gaughran, it works, and some authors put out similar requests on social media too.

Social Media

Most authors would agree that a presence on social media can help build your profile and promote your books. But social media can be used as much more than a promotional platform. It gives authors the opportunity to engage with reviewers, bloggers, and readers directly. A good social media strategy will have you building a network of contacts, fans, and loyal supporters.

It's not unusual for readers to contact authors on social media to say how much they've enjoyed one of their books. If that happens, there's no shame in asking that person if they'd mind putting that compliment in an Amazon review!

Book reviewers

Many book reviewers are active on social media, and post regular links to their blogs. Tracy Shephard is a keen book reviewer, mostly covering fiction. Her blog can be found at www.tracyshephard.wordpress.com

Tracy says, "I'm an avid reader and can read about four books a week. I'm partially disabled so I can't do very much, which means I sit and read a lot. I usually read a book in one sitting. If it doesn't grab me then I read it in about two days."

If Tracy likes a book, then she'll post a review on her blog. She'll also post her review on Amazon.co.uk, on Goodreads, Pinterest, and on Amazon.com. But what if she reads a book and it doesn't appeal to her?

"I have given up on books occasionally - mainly ones I read for the book club I attend. They're books that I wouldn't normally read, so I've given up reviewing these books for my blog. I like to be honest in my reviews and I don't think my negativity is helpful, so I don't review them. I'm sure the books would appeal to other people. They're just not my cup of tea.'

Finding reviewers

You can find book reviewers on Twitter by searching on the term #bookreview. Alternatively, use a search engine, such as Google, to find book reviewers. Different reviewers cover different genres. For example, you can find reviews of fantasy books at www.fantasybookreview.co.uk or children's book at www.bookreviewsformums.co.uk. 'Women on Writing' sometimes reviews books by female writers on www.wow-womenonwriting.com. So find a reviewer sympathetic to your genre and offer them a review copy.

Some authors put a message out on social media, saying their book is available for review, and offer a complementary copy to any potential reviewer. If you're considering this, it's worth knowing that Amazon rules state full disclosure on free reads: "If you received a free product in exchange for your review, please clearly and conspicuously disclose that you received the product free of charge."

Some reviewers, like Tracy, automatically post their reviews onto Amazon. Others, like 'Women on Writing', don't, but they do have a dedicated following of female writers and it's good exposure. Either way, it's good to have reviews of your work appearing in different locations across the world-wide-web.

Goodreads

Goodreads.com has a reviews system which, although prone to misuse like Amazon, is generally used in a positive and constructive manner. Resources on their website include Goodreads Groups, which are lively communities that authors can use to raise awareness of their work and generate reviews.

One of the groups that authors should know about is called, 'Goodreads Authors/Readers'. It's a designated place for authors to connect with readers. You can announce new titles on this forum, request reviews, and post blogs. There are discussion topics dedicated to specific genres, and you can engage with book cover artists and illustrators, editors, publishers, ebook formatters and website designers.

Other groups on Goodreads include 'Classic Horror Lovers', 'Supernatural Fiction Readers', 'Addicted to YA', and 'Paranormal Romance & Urban Fantasy'. The choice of groups is vast, so it pays to be selective.

The discussions within groups are wide ranging, but new releases, favourite authors, recommend-ations, and reading challenges are all covered. The groups can be quite lively, encourage interaction, and generate interest in your work. Some are like joining an online book club, and they provide good opportunities for authors to interact with other people interested in their genre. Find popular groups here: www.goodreads.com/group/popular.

Arrange a book blog tour

Bookmasters.com describes a book blog tour as, "A popular form of online publicity that is worthwhile for all authors. A blog book tour is much like a traditional book tour, except the stops are all virtual. Instead of going from bookstore to bookstore, the author goes from blog to blog."

Tracy Shephard explains, "A blog tour is where a group of book reviewers all get a specific date to tweet their reviews. These blogs sometimes include a Q&A with the author, or whatever the blogger wants to include. If I have a blog tour coming up, I read those books as a priority."

There are many specialist bloggers out there, always interested in new content. Identify blogs that are relevant to your book topic, and see if you can arrange to include them in your blog tour. Motorsport blogs would be perfect if your book is on Formula 1. But if your book is on healthy eating, then health, nutrition, or allergy blogs would be more appropriate. The bloggers you approach don't have to be book reviewers - some might just be interested in an author interview on a relevant topic.

Authors with similar interests might offer you a guest blog on their own site, so be sociable and let other writers know that you're available. Blog book tours can take many different formats, and whether they're reviews or interviews, they always present a good opportunity to get some publicity for your book and other literary works.

Read more about book blog tours here: www.bookmasters.com/blog/blog-book-tour

Chapter 13
Rachel Abbott: "From self-published to best-selling author. Here's how I did it."

Best-selling author, Rachel Abbott, self-published her first novel, *Only the Innocent,* in November 2011, through Kindle Direct Publishing. It sold well, reaching number 1 in the Kindle charts and was the second best-selling self-published title in 2012. Four novels later, she's still enjoying best-seller status.

Rachel explains, "I wrote my first novel to fulfil an

ambition, and never thought about a publishing deal. But when my family read it, they said it was good and I should try to get it published. So I made a half-hearted attempt to get an agent, and a couple replied with some positive feedback. The agents who responded however, felt that my book wasn't the sort of thing that publishers were looking for at the time.

"I'd looked at Kindle as a publishing platform early in 2010 while I was writing the book, but you needed a US bank account, so being a Brit, I decided against it. However, in 2011, six months after getting the positive feedback, I looked into it again, and found things had changed.

"So that September, I published *Only the Innocent* as an ebook for Kindle. The process wasn't as straight forward as it is now – to make sure the layout worked you ideally had to use HTML. Fortunately I had the skills to do that, and published on Amazon without too much difficulty.

"I emailed all my friends and asked them to buy my book, saying I'd pay them back. I started selling the book at £1.99, and was delighted when I sold six on Christmas Day, even though they were probably all sold to friends and family, none of whom actually had a Kindle!

"That Christmas, I got thinking: *I used to market my company to our clients. Why am I not being proactive, marketing my book?*

"So I wrote a marketing plan, 27 pages long, comparable to one I would have presented to the board at work. By the time I published the book, I'd retired, so I was able to spend 14 hours every day implementing my plan. It took three months to do the bulk of the work, making contacts on social media, submitting my book to reviewers, and running promotions, but it didn't end there. The marketing is ongoing and constantly evolving.

"Half way through January 2012, I dropped the price to 99p and promoted it to everyone identified in my marketing plan. On 18th February, my book reached number 1 in the Kindle charts, and it stayed at the top until the middle of March. I was delighted, but I wasn't complacent. I kept marketing the book and was learning new stuff the whole time.

"I didn't know anything about social media, but I started a new blog, approached reviewers, and was very active on Twitter and Facebook. It was a real hard slog, but it paid off.

"On social media, people say you shouldn't put your own books up all the time, but rightly or wrongly, I actually found this approach worked for me. The average Twitter user only logs on for six minutes a day, and some of the top marketing people say you should post almost the same tweet every 20 minutes.

"In the early days, Twitter was very important and amazingly helpful to me. But now I prefer Facebook, as the format seems to encourage a more engaged and supportive following. I use both my private Facebook timeline and my author page to promote my books. Posts on my author page only reach about 16% of followers unless I pay for visibility. So I use the 'Promote Post' facility on Facebook. It's expensive, but worth it for me.

"Marketing is all about visibility, and so counting the cost of these promotions against direct sales is only half of the story. When my book is in a promotion, I probably receive about 49p per copy sold. If I am paying 40p for each click through to the Amazon page in a promotion, it seems hardly worth it – especially as not every click will result in a sale. But these clicks drive the book further up the charts, and so make it more visible, and that in itself results in more sales – ones that I am not paying for through advertising.

"When the price goes up again, my book is higher up the charts, and so benefits from more sales at the full price.

"I also have a blog, which helps raise awareness of my books; I'm not sure it produces vast sales numbers, but it does help with brand recognition. I make sure that my book covers are seen in as many places as possible, because apparently people need to see something seven times, just for them to be aware of it.

"The blog also helps capture names for my reader database, which is a great marketing tool. The best way to get a database of readers is to put a link in the back of your Kindle book, which they can click to sign up to your newsletter. For me, this has worked brilliantly. Use Campaign Monitor, MailChimp or one of the many other applications designed for this purpose to store your data, and to design and send your emails. It helps to streamline the process and keep it simple.

"People can sign up to my newsletter on Facebook too. I run Facebook adverts specifically to get new names and on one occasion I offered 50 signed copies of my books in a prize draw. The promotion got me 3000 names for my database. However, the people who've signed up because they've read a book are twice as likely to click on links in my newsletters than those who entered a competition.

"I now have a number of part-time assistants helping with the marketing. They take care of Twitter, database work, competitions and launch parties. I still produce a new marketing plan every year but now I focus *less* on getting new readers and *more* on making sure I communicate with existing readers.

"I've also put together a database of reviewers so I have all their details in one place. This makes it easy when you've got a new book to promote. I send a professional package giving full details of the book – the cover, the blurb, the length, the genre, etc. I then offer them a Kindle version or a PDF, or in some cases a paperback.

"In 2012, I finally got an agent, Lizzy Kremer at David Higham Associates, who has helped me to sell foreign translation rights to publishers around the world. English language rights remain with me but the agency has now sold rights in twelve different languages.

"That same year, my agent negotiated a publishing deal with Thomas and Mercer in the USA for my first two books. Despite impressive sales in the UK, the books hadn't sold as well in North America, so I wanted to see what a publisher could achieve. I signed a contract for publication in North America, including Canada.

"I was very pleased with Thomas and Mercer, who increased sales in America. When the contract was up for renewal, though, they were interested in World English rights, and I wanted to retain my rights in the UK, so sadly we parted company.

"My third novel, *Sleep Tight*, sold well on both

sides of the Atlantic, so Thomas and Mercer had clearly done an excellent job of raising my profile in the USA. I did enjoy working with the publisher, and certainly wouldn't rule out a publishing deal in the future.

"My subsequent novel, *Stranger Child*, and novella, *Nowhere Child*, both published last year, and were both bestsellers. I've sold almost 1.7 million books since I first self-published in 2011.

"When I started self-publishing in paperback in 2012, I used Createspace. I later switched to Lightning Source because it has extended distribution, shipped from the UK, so bookstores can buy from Lightning Source at a sensible cost. Createspace's extended distribution ships from the USA, which makes it expensive for British bookstores to stock your book.

"While those two services are print-on-demand, I also recently ordered a print run of *Stranger Child*, from Silverwood Books because I wanted British bookstores to be able to buy them for the same price as a traditionally published book, and this seemed the most straightforward way to achieve that.

"I sell more ebooks than print books, but I think that's true of a lot of writers."

Rachel's new book, *Kill Me Again*, is out now in ebook and in paperback formats.

www.rachel-abbott.com

Chapter 14
Jon Rance: "My publisher showed me just how professional I needed to be as an author"

The world of publishing has changed in recent years, with self-publishing losing a lot of its early stigma and becoming a respectable route to publication. Jon Rance is a traditionally published author who's embraced the 'independent' approach.

Jon writes comedy novels about love, life and relationships. His first book, 'This Thirtysomething Life', was snapped up by *Hodder and Stoughton* after he self-published the ebook on Kindle, and it reached number 7 in the Kindle charts. A two-book publishing deal ensued. He's now returned to self publishing, and has just released his fourth novel, Sunday Dinners, and a Christmas novella.

"When my first novel, 'This Thirtysomething Life', got into the Kindle top ten charts, I thought it was a miracle because A: it's self-published and to sell that many books on your own against the might of the professional publishing machine is a huge achievement. B: I literally had no idea what I was doing. C: Unlike a lot of other authors, I didn't do much marketing or self-promotion. Basically, I got lucky.

"This remarkable success was followed by a call from *Hodder and Stoughton*, who offered me a two-book deal. I'd spent the previous five years approaching publishers with my books, only to receive a chorus of resounding 'no's. Yet here was a major player asking me. It was surreal. I soon had an agent and I honestly thought I would soon be the next J.K Rowling!

"Unfortunately, the fairytale ending that I'd envisaged failed to transpire. 'This Thirtysomething Life' was in the top fifty on the Amazon Kindle charts and had previously reached no 7, selling 55,000 copies, but when *Hodder* took over, the ebook's Amazon ranking was taken away and effectively, we had to start again. I'd originally released the book for 99p and it was highly visible to Amazon viewers, but *Hodder* released the book at £4.99, with no marketing and no visibility, which made it very difficult to get back into the charts.

"On the plus side, they sold a significant number of foreign rights deals that helped promote me around the world. Financially, this more than made up for the flagging sales in the UK. In the end, the sales figures were OK and I don't think it's anything that *Hodder* did wrong, but the circumstances of the re-launch gave it little chance of success."

The pricing dilemma

"I think one of the biggest challenges for ebook publishers today is pricing. Back in 2013 when all of this happened, ebooks were just starting to take off, but publishers hadn't caught up. They were charging £2.99+ for ebooks, which meant that self-published authors had a shot at success if we could make a great product and sell it for 99p. Today, of course, a lot of publishers have digital imprints and can charge much less. This means it's much more difficult for self-published authors to get noticed.

"My total sales across all titles are close to 100,000, which sounds like a lot, but to hit the top, you need to be selling twice that many copies of each book - especially when you're only charging 99p. I know a lot of authors refuse to charge less than £2.99, and I wish I could charge that much, but with intense competition, and established authors selling their back catalogue for 99p, independents can't compete. Until you have a huge fan base or a large advance from a publisher (which hardly ever happens) you have to charge less for each book and hope to sell more copies.

"The biggest thing with Amazon is visibility and

the only way to get that, is to get high enough in the charts that your book pops up all over the place. For self-published authors, selling their books cheaply is the easiest way to do well in the charts. If you reach the top 10 or 20, even at 99p you'll make good money and hopefully get new fans, who may be willing to pay more in the future."

Living the dream

"Despite the disappointing sales figures in the UK, I learnt so much from working with *Hodder and Stoughton*, and made some incredible contacts. It was an experience I loved from start to finish. It's every writer's dream to get a publishing deal. The highlights were seeing the paperback copies for the first time, especially when they appeared in bookshops and libraries. I also got to do some brilliant interviews, a Q&A with one of my writing heroes, and I was featured in magazines. Seeing my book in other languages and getting 'fan mail' from across the globe is a feeling I can't describe!

"The lowest point was when my second novel, 'Happy Endings' came out and passed the world by. It's one of the difficult things about publishing. You imagine that when you get a book deal, the publisher will launch a huge marketing campaign, and you'll sell thousands of copies worldwide. The reality, for me, was that there was no big marketing campaign. I had some support - they got interviews and tweeted - but I did most of it myself. It wasn't enough to stop the book from flopping. This was hard for me because I'd worked hard on it, and it's a really good book. It just didn't find an audience. It sold a few thousand copies, but nothing as high as I'd hoped.

It's the sort of book that reduced to 99p, could do very well! Maybe one day it'll be a bestseller!

"I think the best thing about having a publisher is the editorial process. I worked with some incredible people at *Hodder* and they really helped shape my work. Working on a book with professional editors from the start guarantees it will be a better book than if you worked alone. Yes it takes longer, but they definitely help make the book better. They help you work on the characters, plot, structure, and they're always there to bounce ideas off. I'm still friends with my editor at Hodder and she's been a wonderful person to go to for help and advice.

"The other thing publishers offer is a sense of legitimacy. Before I got a publishing deal I found it difficult making contacts and getting interviews. Now, having been published, I've made some real friends, got great contacts, and found so many authors who help and support me."

Jon's return to self-publishing
"When my two-book deal with Hodder and Stougton came to an end, my third and fourth books didn't find a publisher, so I returned to self-publishing because it was the only way to get the new books out there. I'm happy with that. The beauty of working on my own again is that I can work at my own pace.

"Traditional publishing is very slow. Self-publishing gives writers the chance to get their work out faster and create more. One thing I did learn from my time working with editors and professionals is the importance of quality, and I'm not letting that suffer. I still work with a brilliant editor and make sure everything I put out is top quality. I do my own covers. I went to art school and I've always been interested in design. Covers have to be professional and hopefully mine are.

"Working with *Hodder and Stougton* was a fascinating and eye-opening experience. Looking back on 'This Thirtysomething Life' I should have got it professionally edited before I published it. I would never publish a book now without getting it edited."

The demands on a modern author

"Being an author is so much more than writing books. It's about promotion and becoming a social media expert and if you aren't prepared to put all the work in, then you aren't going to make it. I find Twitter is a great way of getting the word out there. I think the most successful marketing tool though, is the network of friends I've made. When I have a new book coming out, bloggers and authors I've met always help me. So if I had some advice for aspiring writers, it would be to make friends. Help others and they will help you.

"I don't enjoy the interviews and marketing as much as I do writing, but I know it's a huge part of what being a modern author is. Getting your book read (no matter how good it is) is the hardest part and if no-one knows who you are, it's even harder.

"Self-publishing is saturated at the moment and I think working with a digital publisher is the way forward. If you look at the Amazon Kindle charts, the number of self-published books doing well is in decline. I'm hoping that down the line I'll get another publishing deal and then hopefully more ebooks and paperbacks will follow."

"I'm starting work on my first rom-com novel

soon, and I'm looking to find a publisher for this: perhaps *Bookouture, Carina* or *Harper Impulse*, because they're working with new and exciting authors."

www.jonrance.com

Chapter 15
Charles Naton: "Being fashionably obscure can actually be an advantage"

Getting a book deal is every new author's dream, right? Why then, are so many traditionally published authors now choosing the independent route? Charles Naton shares his experiences.

Charles Naton is the author of 'Section 12', a wartime psychological horror, telling the story of a traumatised WWII soldier, who ends up in an

English psychiatric clinic after D-Day. He experiences headaches, nightmares, and supernatural phenomenon. Charles' dramatic supernatural tale was originally published through the small publisher, *Can Write Will Write*. He's since self-published the book and its sequel, entitled 'The Cronus Equation', which came out in May 2016.

Charles explains, "My first step into publishing was when *Can Write Will Write* offered me a book deal. It was a new venture and we didn't know each other, so I only signed a contract for the e-publishing rights initially. The publisher gave me some very useful editorial feedback, which was a great help in the early days. It taught me to look at my own work through the eyes of an editor as opposed to an author. I agreed to do my fair share of marketing, as they're a small publisher, and was committed to the project.

"Then things started to go wrong when I saw the cover design they'd produced. I hated it. This left me stuck in the strange situation of being reluctant to throw my weight behind my own work! I was also bewildered by the publisher's reluctance to make the book available on Amazon. I thought it was a poor business decision not to have any kind of presence on that mega-platform.

"So, keenly aware that one never gets a second chance to make a first impression, I made a conscious decision to draw as little attention to myself and my work as possible, until I got my electronic rights back, and could republish on my own terms. I wrote the sequel while I watched the clock ticking down!"

"Following that disappointing experience, I wanted complete control over the publishing process, so I set up my own publishing company, *Cortlandt Publications*. This enabled me to control my own ISBN series, which is important to me. What many publishers neglect to mention is that although you may own your material, they own any ISBN they allocate to your work. Sure, you can republish with a different number, but the fewer ISBNs there are swirling around your work the better. Nothing succeeds like simplicity. There are a few hoops to jump through to get your own ISBN series from Nielson in the UK, but it's not really the impossible mystery that some publishers would have you believe."

The relaunch

"When I got my rights back, I relaunched the book with a new cover, making it available in paperback too. The good news is that since striking out on my own, I've seen a significant rise in interest and in sales. At the moment I'm focusing more on building my reputation rather than shifting volume. That takes time and a lot of shoe leather if you're working by yourself.

"Doing it all myself has been a real education. I've learned an awful lot about the subtleties of print layout - a couple of millimetres here and there can really enhance the reading experience. I urge any self-publishers to resist the temptation to cram their work into as few pages as possible to save a little bit on each sale. The thing to remember is that a book is more than just the words it contains. The way it looks and feels is just as important as what's printed inside.

"I've done all my own techy stuff too. I built my

own website, although the artwork was supplied by my long-suffering and extremely talented graphic artist. I own the domain, rent the server space and I manage my own affairs. It all costs about a fiver a month. I don't have any kind of formal IT background, but there are a ton of really good drag-and-drop web design programs available, and they needn't be hugely expensive. I tend to pick up software when it's on offer if I think I might have a future need for it. I think of it as an apprentice building up his toolkit. I seldom pay any more than £50 for software, and that policy has really paid off as there's not much I can't do for myself these days.

"I've also learnt how to collaborate with other creative folk, to listen to their specialist insight, and explain important decisions where it's not possible to please everyone. Self-publishing is a big challenge, but it's something I enjoy doing. I like figuring out how to do things and get the best results. It was a challenge finding the right graphic artist to represent my work. Sure, there are lots of very talented and capable people out there, but the trick is finding that one that's right for you. Add print quality issues, IT issues, distribution, ISBN allocation and marketing into the mix and the serious self-publisher ends up being very busy indeed."

The advantage in obscurity
"Since deciding to self-publish, I've found word of mouth, via the internet, is the most successful way to sell books. Being fashionably obscure can actually be an advantage. Rightly or wrongly, one of the by-products of the modern post-industrial era is a huge surplus of mistrust. Consumers instinctively mistrust

the large and opaque corporations that supply them, and in their turn, corporations mistrust increasingly vociferous and litigious consumers. This mutual mistrust has given birth to what I like to call 'a subculture of the small'.

"This is expressed through counterculture campaigns to shop local and support 'independent' artists and content producers. As one of these 'independent' producers I am more accessible to readers and seemingly less tainted by that low hanging cloud of suspicion that often hovers over large commercial enterprises.

"At this early stage in my career, I have the ability to engage with readers and customers at a very personal level, which simply isn't possible for established household names, no matter how much they might wish to do so. Thus a reader looking for something 'authentic', which is not the obvious product of a focus group algorithm, will gravitate towards authors like myself.

"This consumer outlook and market dynamic can be seen in literature, art, music and increasingly in cyberspace. For every dozen or so happy consumers in the mass-market, there is at least one disenchanted soul searching for something else, something 'real'. That's still an awfully big potential audience, but of course the trick is finding them and gaining their trust."

Marketing and reaching new readers

"I do all my own marketing and have learnt to be very adaptable. Obviously reader reviews and recommendations are an excellent tool, although you have to be prepared to step back from those. They belong to the readers, not the author.

"It's important to let the customer lead the marketing. By that I mean you have to be prepared to abandon that lovingly prepared and foolproof marketing plan when you discover that all the action's happening somewhere else! I'd prepared an excellent Google campaign and spent a great deal of time on SEO work, only to discover that my future readers were all hanging out on Facebook and Amazon. Amazon's Kindle library has been one of the best ways for new readers to find and try out previously unknown authors like myself. Half a dozen signed books donated to cosy pubs around the country have done me no harm either."

"As for buying in specialist skills, I'd suggest that if you can do a good job yourself, then do it. If you need a specialist skill such as a designer or webmaster, remember you get what you pay for. Make sure you understand exactly what you're buying before you commit, and if you see a 'guaranteed formula for success' then run in the opposite direction!"

"We are living in fascinating times, where it's possible to take an idea and reach out to literally millions of potential customers in ways that were never possible before. However, self-publishing still requires a lot of hard work, in addition to actually writing something good in the first place! Self-publishing isn't for everyone and the results will be hugely disappointing if you're hoping to be an overnight success, but for the able, the committed and the determined, it really can be a brave new world."

www.charlesnaton.com

Chapter 16
The art of marketing yourself and your work

So you're a keen writer; perhaps writing stories and articles. Or perhaps you have an unpublished book manuscript gathering dust in a cupboard somewhere.

Do you want to get more of your work published? Sell more books? Perhaps you're unsure where to begin? Here are some simple things you can do to market yourself and increase your chances of success!

Freelance writing can be a slow and unpredictable business, with long time lags between sending your idea to a publisher, editor, or agent, and securing that writing assignment or book deal. So if you're serious about being published, you need to pitch ideas regularly, especially in the world of magazine publishing.

Do you have existing contacts in publishing? If so, stay in touch. Some editors will tell you if they're looking for specific types of article or story. When I started writing magazine articles for a living, one editor told me that if I could secure an interview with two druids, she'd buy the story. I spent the rest of that month trying to get druids to talk. They're a private bunch and I could understand why she'd had a problem! But eventually I found two druids willing to cooperate. The rest is history!

Even if you don't have a compelling article idea, do stay in touch with editors you know, because they might have themed editions coming up, or just have an assignment in mind that would suit you! After I'd been freelancing for a couple of years, I started getting more commissions without having to ask for them.

Get a website

Every serious writer needs a website to showcase their work. My simple website has led to a range of writing assignments, including a book deal. I've received an enquiry about ghosting someone's memoir too, but I didn't take that one up due to their low budget. The point is, my website generates work.

So if you don't already have a website, it's worthwhile building one. There are many free sites offering the tools to build your own. A website doesn't have to be expensive or onerous. A simple site will get you started and it will evolve over time.

Before you get started, it's a good idea to browse other writers' websites to get a feel for the kind of look, feel, and content that you want to include. Think about your colour scheme, navigation bar, how you want to present yourself, and what downloads you want to make available. You might want to include some of the following:

- An 'About me' page
- A list of some of your clients
- Details of your books, with links to Amazon
- Samples of your articles
- Links to online stories you've written
- A link to your blog
- Links to your social media pages
- A list of the services you offer
- Testimonials from editors

- Examples of your photography
- Contact details
- An image of yourself.

Among the many free website building tools available online are the ones listed below. Explore the options and choose one that you find most intuitive or appealing.

- Wix: www.wix.com
- Yola: www.yola.com
- Webs: www.webs.com
- Weebly: www.weebly.com
- Moon Fruit: www.moonfruit.com
- Google Sites: www.sites.google.com

Social media

Many authors swear by social media. I used it initially to promote my books. Now I use it more to find interviewees and interesting subjects to write about. Just browsing Twitter can give me story ideas!

Authors use a mix of approaches for getting people to notice them on social media. Novelist Carole Matthews asked her twitter followers to "RT to win a signed copy of The Cake Shop in the Garden," every Wednesday evening, when the Great British Bake Off was on TV! It resulted in her tweets going viral and she announced the winner in the morning!

Other authors offer free samples, special offers, giveaways, competitions, and prize draws to generate interest in their work. Social media expert, Ken Krogue who founded InsideSales.com, writes on Forbes.com, "Headlines with numbers in them consistently perform well". So 'Ten steps to becoming a paid writer,' might be a winner in terms of generating click throughs. Ken also suggests posting 'how to' articles on social media, because they get a good response. Two #hashtags in each tweet are optimal he says. They make your post more visible in searches.

You might be sceptical about the value of social media. It can be a huge distraction from actually writing, but some authors swear it helps them sell books. Derek Haines, who writes the Just Publishing Advice Blog says, "Put simply, the more I tweet my books, the more books I sell. A simple fact that proves that Twitter spam works!"

On another level, constant spamming can be annoying, so there's a balance to be struck. Personally I find engaging with people online, and getting involved in conversations, is more likely to make people interested in my books, than constant suggestions that they "Buy My Book!"

So what's the key to successful engagement on social media? Try to identify what your audience enjoy and value. Give them lots of it, and invite them to be interactive and engage with you. Ken Krogue adds, you should, "listen with two ears and one mouth". Listen to what your followers are saying and engage with them.

Blogs

Some authors promote themselves and their books by blogging regularly. This is often more effective and engaging for followers than a hard sell on book titles. Novelist, Chris Hill, does this well, writing articles including 'The Double Life of An Author,' and 'Do Authors Need a Brand?' on his blog.

The biggest challenge for many new bloggers however, is getting readers. Let your social media followers know when you have a new blog post, and send an email link to any friends or family who might be interested. Many authors use blogging sites such as www.wordpress.com or www.blogger.com, to write blogs that help promote their book. Some authors say they don't have time for blogging, but others are certain that it helps them sell books.

Blogging expert, Ruth Holroyd says, "Don't let your blog become a burden. Do it because you enjoy it, and if you don't enjoy it, don't do it!"

Other approaches to marketing

You can engage in numerous other activities to raise your profile and market yourself and your book. Talks, book launches, and book signings can be a great way to sell books, but don't be despondent if sales are slow. It happens to us all. Even JK Rowling experienced disappointments and set backs during her early writing career!

Try to arrange local radio interviews, notify the local press that you've had a book published, send them a press release about it, and do a prize draw, inviting people to sign up to your author newsletter. This will help you build an email list of potential readers. Keep people on your mailing list up to date with new releases. Write articles about your newly published books for local magazines, and circulate review copies to people who have said they're willing to review your work online or in print.

Marketing yourself to magazines and newspapers is a more direct affair. You need to pitch ideas directly to editors to win commissions. It can't do any harm to build a wider reputation for yourself as an expert in your chosen subject too. Then you might pick up work with PR agencies and content producers. I had a call from a PR agency because my website says I write pet articles. They needed an article for an insurance company about holiday cottages that take dogs. That was another assignment in the bag from a PR company I'd never even heard of!

Obviously, it makes sense to always deliver brilliant copy on time and to specification, be prepared to amend it if they don't like your first attempt. You'll soon learn the style that each client prefers. Having a book published can also add to your credibility and may help to establish you as an expert in your chosen field.

Most important of all, is don't give up. You have to be persistent and keep on looking for opportunities. Good luck.

Chapter 17
What next?

So you've reached the end of *The Little Book of Freelance Writing*. I hope it's inspired you, given you some ideas and the confidence to try some new things.

What are you going to do now? Try those pitching techniques discussed in Chapter 3? Start a blog? Perhaps experiment with self-publishing?

Wherever you go from here, remember that as writers, we're all on a journey. We all experience ups and downs, set-backs and successes. You will receive rejections. I do too. And there will be times when it seems hopeless, but if you persevere, it can be very rewarding. Publishing is a very competitive marketplace, but for the determined writer, there is also a wealth of opportunity.

Modern technology has opened up publishing to everyone, and it needn't cost you anything. If you're struggling to get recognition from traditional publishers, then the emergence of e-books and print-on-demand self-publishing means that you can proceed without them. That's amazing.

It's worth remembering that big sales by independent authors are usually accompanied by dedicated marketing campaigns. Many writers do talks locally which helps them sell books.

Whichever route you choose, success takes commitment and hard work, but the barriers to entry are now very low and the costs are low. So what have you got to lose? Let your imagination fly.

Good luck!

Thank You For Reading.
I Hope You Enjoyed This Book.
Please Consider Leaving A Review On Amazon.

*   *   *

More titles by the same author...

Freelance Writing: Aim Higher, Earn More by Susie Kearley.

In 2011 Susie Kearley quit a career in marketing to follow her lifelong dream of becoming a full-time freelance writer. She had no contacts, no real experience in the publishing industry, and no idea whether she would succeed. Yet through sheer tenacity, determination and hard work, she built a solid career as a freelance writer, in the middle of a global economic recession. Today, she works for some well-known publications and earns a living from her writing.

In this book, Susie discusses her approaches to getting published and answers many of the burning questions asked of any freelance writer:

- How much money do writers make? How much do you earn?
- How can I generate more income from my writing?
- Where can I find the best opportunities in freelance writing?
- How can I learn from rejection and increase my chances of success?
- How do I break into magazines and newspapers overseas?
- Do I need an agent? What can they do for me?
- What's it like working with a small press book publisher?
- What are the biggest challenges to a sustainable freelance career, and how can I overcome them?

This book discusses writers' average earnings and the many challenges facing someone following a freelance career. It explains how to generate income from feature articles, blogging, books, photography, and content creation for business. It details the money to be made from associations that pay out secondary royalties on your articles, photographs, and books. It also looks at record keeping and organisational skills - essential requirements once your workload reaches a certain level.

This book is written for those writers who've seen modest successes in publishing, to help them take their writing to the next level. It will help anyone looking for new inspiration and insight, who wants to earn more from their writing.

There are many beginners books on the market. This book is different. It focuses on making a regular income from writing. It doesn't go into great detail on the basics like how to pitch, because that's covered in lots of other books, including the author's first book, Freelance Writing on Health, Food and Gardens.

Part 1 focuses on different ways of making money from your writing.

Part 2 looks at working for magazines around the world and discusses the things you need to think about when you write for overseas markets.

Part 3 looks at opportunities in book publishing, a day in court, professional indemnity insurance, marketing, social media and writing as therapy.

First published: January 2015.

Freelance Writing on Health, Food and Gardens by Susie Kearley.

In 2011 Susie Kearley quit a 15 year marketing career to start up as a freelance writer in the middle of a recession. In this book, she shares how, in under two years, she went from being an aspirational rookie, to working for some of the biggest names in publishing. She explains how:

- She built up valuable contacts from nothing;
- She used her nutrition qualifications and background in natural health to spur her career forward;
- She generated numerous feature ideas from single opportunities;
- She sold articles on health, food and gardening topics to diverse and unexpected markets;
- Her unrelenting perseverance and tenacity came good in the end, despite numerous obstacles;
- She challenged those who said she would never succeed and proved them wrong.

This book is inspirational. It provides valuable tips to get you started in writing for the health, food and gardening markets, and has wider relevance to other fields of journalism.

Interviews with other writers - all working in the health, food and gardening markets - give superb insight into the highlights and challenges that each of them have faced in this field of work. The book features interviews with some well-known writers and with others who are still building their reputation, including:

- Amanda Hamilton, celebrity nutritionist and health writer;
- Jackie Lynch, nutritionist and health writer;
- Nick Baines, travel writer focusing on food topics;
- Sue Ashworth, food and cookery writer;
- John Negus, gardening writer;
- Helen Riches, garden designer and writer.

Each of these professionals offers their own hints for getting published in their specialist markets.

Susie provides humorous accounts of the obstacles she faced, as well as tips on how to write a winning pitch, how to market yourself as a writer, and how to avoid legal issues. She provides anecdotes and personal insights that many freelance writers will relate to, on topics from getting paid, to quashing the myths of freelance writing.

This book is a valuable resource for anyone wanting to be a successful freelance writer in the health, food, and gardening markets.

First published on 28 February 2014 by Compass Books.

16400220R00060

Printed in Poland
by Amazon Fulfillment
Poland Sp. z o.o., Wrocła